OF HEAVEN AND HELL

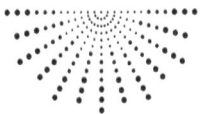

JACOB BEHMEN

Translated by
REVEREND WILLIAM LAW'S

ALICIA ÉDIIONS

CONTENTS

Préface   1
OF HEAVEN AND HELL   2
THE LIFE OF JACOB BEHMEN   46

*D*ear Reader,

If thou wilt use these Words aright, and art in good Earnest, *thou shalt certainly find the Benefit thereof. But I desire thou mayest be warned, if thou art not* in Earnest, *not to meddle with the* dear Names of God, *in and by which the most* High Holiness *is invoked, moved, and powerfully desired, lest they kindle the* Anger of God *in thy Soul. For we must not abuse the* Holy Names of God. *This little Book is only for those that would fain* repent, *and are in a* Desire to begin. *Such will find what Manner of Words therein, and whence they are* born. *Be you herewith commended to the* Eternal Goodness *and* Mercy of God.

OF HEAVEN AND HELL

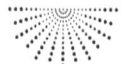

A DIALOGUE BETWEEN A SCHOLAR AND
HIS MASTER

by Jacob Behmen (Jakob Boehme)
1575-1624, The Teutonic Theosopher

SHOWING

Whither the blessed and the damned Souls go when they depart from their Bodies;

and How Heaven and Hell are in Man;

Where the Angels and Devils dwell in this World's Time;

How far Heaven and Hell are asunder;

and What and Whence the Angels and Human Souls are;

What the Body of Man is; and Why the Soul is capable of receiving Good and Evil;

Of the Destruction of the World;

Of Man's Body in and after the Resurrection; Where Heaven and Hell shall be;

Of the Last Judgement; and Why the Strife in the Creature must be.

Composed by a Soul that loveth all who are *Children* of JESUS CHRIST, under the *Cross*.

A DIALOGUE between
JUNIUS, a SCHOLAR,
and THEOPHORUS, his MASTER

The Scholar asked his Master, saying;

Whither goeth the Soul when the Body dieth?

His master answered him;

There is no Necessity for it to go any whither.

What not! said the inquisitive Junius:

Must not the Soul leave the Body at Death, and go either to Heaven or Hell?

It needs no going forth, replied the venerable Theophorus:

Only the outward mortal Life with the Body shall separate themselves from the Soul. The Soul hath Heaven and Hell within itself before, according as it is written, "**The Kingdom of God cometh not with Observation, neither shall they say,** Lo here! or Lo there! For **behold the Kingdom of God is within you**." And which soever of the two, that is, either Heaven or Hell is manifested in it, in that the Soul standeth.

Here Junius said to his Master;

This is hard to understand. Doth it not enter into Heaven or Hell, as a Man entereth into a House; or as one goeth through a Hole or Casement, into an unknown Place; so goeth it not into another World?

The Master spoke and said;

No. There is verily no such Kind of entering in; forasmuch as Heaven and Hell are everywhere, being universally co-extended.

How is that possible? *said the Scholar.*

What, can Heaven and Hell be here present, where we are now sitting? And if one of them might, can you make me believe that both should ever be here together?

Then spoke the Master in this Manner:

I have said that Heaven is everywhere present; and it is true. For God is in Heaven; and God is everywhere. I have said also, that Hell must be in like Manner everywhere; and that is also true. For the **wicked One**, who is the Devil, is in Hell; and the whole World, as the Apostle hath taught us, lieth in the **wicked One**, or the **evil One;** which is as much as to say, not only that the Devil is in the World, but also that the World is in the Devil; and if in the Devil, then in Hell too, because he is there. So Hell therefore is everywhere, as well as Heaven; which is the Thing that was to be proved.

The Scholar, startled hereat, said,

Pray make me to understand this.

To whom the Master said:

Understand then what Heaven is: **It is but the Turning in of the Will into the Love of God**. Wheresoever thou findest God manifesting Himself in Love, there thou findest Heaven, without travelling for it so much as one Foot. And by this understand also what Hell is, and where it is. I say unto thee, it is **but the Turning in of the Will into the Wrath of God**. Wheresoever the Anger of God doth more or less manifest itself, there certainly is more or less of Hell, in whatsoever Place it be. So that it is but the Turning in of thy Will either into His Love, or into His Anger; and thou art accordingly either in Heaven or in Hell. Mark it well. And this now cometh to pass in this present Life, whereof St.Paul speaking, saith, "**Our Conversation is in Heaven**." And the Lord Christ saith also; " **My Sheep HEAR my Voice, and I know them, and they follow me, and I give them the Eternal Life; and none shall pluck them out of my Hand.**" Observe, he saith not, **I will give** them - after this Life is ended; but **I give** them, that is, **now** - in the Time of this Life. And what else is this Gift of Christ to His Followers but an Eternity of Life; which for certain, can be nowhere but in Heaven. And also if Christ be certainly in Heaven, and they who follow Him in the Regeneration are in His Hand, then are they where He is, and so cannot be out of Heaven: Yea, moreover none shall be able to pluck them out of Heaven, because it is He who holdeth them there, and they are in His Hand which nothing can resist. All therefore doth consist in the Turning in, or Entering of the Will into Heaven, by HEARING the Voice of Christ, and both **Knowing** Him and **Following** Him. And so on the contrary it is also. Understandest thou this?

His Scholar said to him;

I think, in part, I do. But how cometh this entering of the Will into Heaven to pass?

The Master answered him;

This then I will endeavour to satisfy thee in; but thou must be very attentive to what I shall say unto thee. Know then, my Son, that when the Ground of the Will yieldeth itself up to God, then it sinketh out of its own SELF, and out of and beyond all Ground and Place that is or can be imagined, into a certain unknown Deep, where God only is manifest, and where He only worketh and willeth. And then it becometh nothing to itSELF, as to its OWN Working and Willing; and so God worketh and willeth in it. And God dwells in this resigned Will; by which the soul is sanctified, and so fitted to come into Divine Rest. Now in this Case when the Body breaketh, the Soul is thoroughly penetrated all over with the Divine Love, and so thoroughly illuminated with the Divine Light, even as a glowing hot Iron is by the Fire, by which being penetrated throughout, it loseth its Darkness and becometh bright and shining. Now this is t**he Hand of**

Christ, where God's Love thoroughly inhabiteth the Soul, and is in it a shining Light, and a new glorious Life. And then the Soul is in Heaven, and is a Temple of the Holy Ghost, and is itself the very Heaven of God, wherein He dwelleth. Lo, this is the entering of the Will into Heaven and how it cometh to pass.

Be pleased, Sir, to proceed, *said the Scholar,*

and let me know how it fareth on the other Side.

The Master said:

The godly Soul, you see, is in the **Hand of Christ**, that is in Heaven, as He Himself hath told us; and in what Manner this cometh to be so, you have also heard. But the ungodly Soul is not willing in this Lifetime to come into the Divine Resignation of its Will, or to enter into the Will of God; but goeth on still in its OWN Lust and Desire, in Vanity and Falsehood, and so entereth into the Will of the Devil. It receiveth thereupon into itSELF nothing but Wickedness; nothing but Lying, Pride, Covetousness, Envy, and Wrath; and thereinto it giveth up its Will and whole Desire. This is the Vanity of the Will; and this same Vanity or vain Shadow must also in like Manner be manifested in the Soul, which hath yielded up itself to be its Servant; and must work therein, even as the Love of God worketh in the regenerated Will, and penetrates it all over, as Fire doth Iron.

And it is not possible for this Soul to come into the **Rest of God**; because God's Anger is manifested in it, and worketh in it. Now when the Body is parted from this Soul, then beginneth the Eternal Melancholy and Despair; because it now findeth that it is become altogether Vanity, even a Vanity most vexatious to itself, and a distracting Fury, and a self-tormenting Abomination. Now it perceiveth itself disappointed of every Thing which it had before fancied, and blind, and naked, and wounded, and hungry, and thirsty; without the least Prospect of being ever relieved, or Obtaining so much as one Drop of Water of Eternal Life. And it feeleth itself to be a mere Devil to itself, and to be its own Vile Executioner and Tormentor; and is affrighted at its own ugly dark Form, appearing as a most hideous and monstrous Worm, and fain would flee from itself, if it could, but it cannot, being fast bound with the Chains of the Dark Nature, whereinto it had sunk itself when in the Flesh. And so not having learned nor accustomed itself to sink down into the Divine Grace, and being also strongly possessed with the Idea of God, as an Angry and Jealous God, the poor Soul is both afraid and ashamed to bring its Will into God, by which Deliverance might possibly come to it.

The Soul is afraid to do it, as Fearing to be consumed by so doing, under the Apprehension of the Deity as a mere **devouring Fire**. The Soul is also **ashamed** to do it, as being confounded at its own Nakedness and Monstrosity; and therefore would, if it were possible, hide itself from the Majesty of God, and cover its abominable Form from His most holy Eye, though by casting itself still deeper into the Darkness, wherefore then it **will not** enter into God; nay, it cannot enter with its false Will; yea, though it should strive to enter, yet it cannot enter into the Love, because of the Will which hath reigned in it. For such a Soul is thereby captivated in the Wrath; yea , is itself but **mere Wrath**, having by its false Desire, which it had awakened in itself, comprehended and shut up itself therewith, and so transformed itself into the Nature and Property thereof.

And since also the Light of God doth not shine in it, nor the Love of God incline it, the Soul is moreover a **great Darkness**, and is withal an anxious **Fire-Source**, carrying about a Hell within itself, and not being able to discern the least Glimpse of the Light of God, or to feel the least Spark of His love. Thus it dwelleth in itself as in Hell, and needeth no entering into Hell at all, or being carried thither; for in what Place soever it may be, so long as it is in itSELF, it is in the Hell. And though it should travel far, and cast itself many hundred thousand Leagues from its present Place, to be out of Hell; yet still would it remain in the Hellish Source and Darkness.

If this be so, how then cometh it, *said the Scholar to Theophorus*, that a Heavenly Soul doth not in the Time of this Life perfectly perceive the Heavenly Light and Joy; and the Soul which is without God in the World, doth not also here feel Hell, as well as hereafter? Why should they not both be perceived and felt as well in this Life as in the next, seeing that both of them are in Man, and one of them (as you have shown) worketh in every Man?

To whom Theophorus presently returneth this Answer:

The Kingdom of Heaven is in the Saints operative and manifestative of itself by **Faith**. They who carry God within them, and live by His Spirit, find the **Kingdom of God** in their **Faith**; and they feel the Love of God in their **Faith**, by which the Will hath given up it SELF into God, and is made Godlike. In a Word, all is transacted within them **by Faith**, which is to them the Evidence of the Eternal Invisibles, and a great Manifestation in their Spirit of this Divine Kingdom, which is within them. But their natural Life is nevertheless encompassed with Flesh and Blood; and this Standing in a Contrariety thereto, and being placed through the Fall in the Principle of God's Anger, and surrounded about with the World, which by no Means can be reconciled to Faith, these faithful Souls cannot but be very much exposed to Attacks from this World, wherein they are Sojourners; neither can they be insensible of their being thus compassed about with Flesh and Blood, and with this World's vain Lust, which ceaseth not continually to penetrate the outward mortal Life, and to tempt them in manifold Ways, even as it did Christ. Whence the World on one side, and Devil on the other, not without the Curse of God's Anger in Flesh and Blood, do thoroughly penetrate and sift the Life; whereby it cometh to pass that the Soul is often in Anxiety when these three are all set upon it together, and when Hell thus assaulteth the Life, and would manifest itself in the Soul. But the Soul hereupon sinketh down into the Hope of the Grace of God, and standeth like a beautiful Rose in the Midst of Thorns, until the Kingdom of this World shall fall from it in the Death of the Body; And then the Soul first becometh truly manifest in the Love of God, and in His Kingdom, which is the Kingdom of Love; having henceforth nothing more to hinder it. But during this Life she must walk with Christ in this World; and then Christ delivereth her out of her own Hell, by penetrating her with His Love throughout, and standing by her in Hell, and even changing her Hell into Heaven.

But in that thou moreover sayest, why do not the Souls which are without God feel Hell in this World? I answer; They bear it about with them in their wicked Consciences, but they know it not; because the World hath put out their Eyes, and its deadly Cup hath cast them likewise into a Sleep, a most fatal Sleep. Notwithstanding which it must be owned that the Wicked do frequently feel Hell within them during the Time of this mortal Life, though they may not apprehend that it is Hell, because of the earthly Vanity which cleaveth unto them from without, and the sensible Pleasures and Amusements wherewith they are intoxicated. And moreover it is to be noted, that the outward Life in every such one hath yet the Light of the outward Nature, which ruleth in that Life; and so the Pain of Hell cannot, so long as that hath Rule, be revealed.

But when the Body dieth or breaketh away, so as the Soul cannot any longer enjoy such temporal Pleasure and Delight, nor the Light of this outward World, which is wholly thereupon extinguished as to it; then the Soul stands in a eternal Hunger and Thirst after such Vanities as it was here in Love withal, but yet can reach nothing but that false Will, which it had impressed in itself while in the Body; and wherein it had abounded to its great Loss. And now whereas it had too much of its Will in this Life, and yet was not contented therewith, it hath after this Separation by Death, as little of it; which createth in it an everlasting Thirst after that which it can henceforth never more obtain, and causeth it to be in a perpetual anxious Lust after Vanity, according to its former Impression, and in a continual Rage of Hunger after those Sorts of Wickedness and Lewdness whereinto it was immersed, while being in the Flesh.

Fain would it do more Evil still, but that it hath not either wherein or wherewith to effect the Same, left to it; and therefore it doth perform this only **in itself**. All is now internally transacted, as if it were outward; and so the Ungodly Soul is tormented by those Furies which are in his own Mind, and begotten upon himself by himself. For he is verily become his own Devil and Tormentor; and that by which he sinned here, when the Shadow of this World is passed away, abideth still with him in the Impression, and is made his Prison and his Hell. But this hellish Hunger and Thirst cannot be fully manifested in the Soul, till the Body which ministered to the Soul what it lusted after, and with which the Soul was so bewitched, as to dote thereupon, and pursue all its Cravings, be stripped off from it.

I perceive then, *said Junius to his Master,*

that the Soul having played the Wanton with the Body in all Voluptuousness, and having served the Lusts thereof during this Life, retaineth still the very same Inclinations and Affections which it had before; so that when it hath no more Opportunity nor Capacity to satisfy them; and when it finds it cannot, then Hell will open in that Soul, which before had been shut up, by Means of the outward Life in the Body, and of the Light of this World. Do I rightly understand?

Theophorus said,

It is very rightly understood by you. Go on.

On the other hand, *the Scholar went on,*

I clearly perceive by what I have heard, that Heaven

cannot but be in a loving Soul, which is possessed of God, and hath subdued thereby the Body to the Obedience of the Spirit in all Things, and perfectly immersed itself into the Will and Love of God. And when the Body dieth, and this Soul is hence redeemed from the Earth, it is now evident to me, that the Life of God which was hidden in it, will display Itself gloriously, and Heaven will consequently be then manifested. But notwithstanding, if there be not also a local Heaven besides, and a local Hell, I am still at a loss where to place no small Part of the Creation, if not the greatest. For where must all the intellectual Inhabitants abide?

In their own Principle, *answered the Master,*

whether it be of Light or of Darkness. For every created intellectual Being remaineth in its Deeds and Essences, in its Wonders and Properties, in its Life and Image; and therein it beholdeth and feeleth God, as Who is everywhere, whether it be in the Love, or in the Wrath.

If it be in the Love of God, then beholdeth it God accordingly, and feeleth Him as He is Love. But if it hath captivated itself in the Wrath of God, then it cannot behold God otherwise than in the wrathful Nature, nor perceive Him otherwise than as an incensed and vindictive Spirit. All Places are alike to it, if it be in God's Love; and if it be not there, every Place is Hell alike. What Place can bound a Thought? Or what needeth any understanding Spirit to be kept here or there, in order to its Happiness or Misery? Verily, wheresoever it is, it is in the **abyssal** World, where there is neither End nor Limit. And whither, I pray, should it go? Since though it should go a thousand Miles off, or a thousand Times ten thousand Miles, and this ten thousand Times over, beyond the Bounds of the Universe, and into the imaginary Spaces above the Stars, yet it were then still in the very same Point from whence it went out. For God is **the Place** of **Spirit**; if it may be lawful to attribute to Him such a Name, to which the Body hath a Relation: And in God there is no Limit; both near and afar off is here all one; and be it in His Love, or be it in His Anger, the **abyssal Will** of the Spirit is altogether unconfined. It is swift as Thought, passing through all Things; it is magical, and nothing corporeal or from without can let or obstruct it; it dwelleth in its Wonders, and they are its House.

Thus it is with every Intellectual, whether of the Order of Angels, or of human Souls; and you need not fear but there will be Room enough for them all, be they ever so many; and such also as shall best suit them, even according to their Election and Determination; and which may thence very well be called his **own Place**.

At which, *said the Scholar;*

I remember, indeed, that it is written concerning the great Traitor, that he went after Death to **his own Place**.

The Master here said:

The same is true of every Soul, when it departeth this mortal Life: And it is true in like Manner of every Angel, or Spirit whatsoever; which is necessarily determined by its own Choice. As God is everywhere, so also the Angels are everywhere; but each one in its own Principle, and in its own Property, or (if you had rather) in **its own Place**. The same Essence of God, which is a Place of Spirits, is confessed to be everywhere; but the Appropriation, or Participation thereof is different to every one, according as each hath attracted magically in the Earnestness of the Will. The same Divine Essence which is with the Angels of God above, is with us also below: And the same Divine Nature which is with us, is likewise with them; but after different Manners and in different Degrees, communicated and participated.

And what I have said here of the **Divine**, is no less to be considered by you in the Participation of the Diabolical Essence and Nature, which is the **Power of Darkness**, as to the manifold Modes, Degrees, and Appropriations thereof in the false Will. In this World there is Strife between them: but when this World hath reached in any one the Limit, then the Principle catcheth that which is its own: and so the Soul receiveth Companions accordingly, that is, either Angels or Devils.

To whom the Scholar said again:

Heaven and Hell then being in us at Strife in the

Time of this Life, and God Himself being also thus near unto us, where can Angels and Devils dwell?

And the Master answered him thus:

Where thou dost not dwell as to thy **SELF-hood**, and to thine **OWN Will**, there the holy Angels dwell with thee, and everywhere all over round about thee. Remember this well. On the contrary, where thou dwellest as to thySELF, in SELF-Seeking, and SELF-Will, there to be sure the Devils will be with thee, and will take up their abode with thee, and dwell all over thee, and round about thee everywhere. Which God in his Mercy prevent.

I understand not this, *said the Scholar,*

so perfectly well as I could wish. Be pleased to make it a little more clear to me.

The Master then spoke:

Mark well what I am going to say. Where the Will of God in any Thing willeth, there is God manifested; and in this very manifestation of God, the

Angels do dwell. But where God in any Creature willeth not with the Will of that Creature, there God is not manifested to it, neither can He be; but dwelleth in Himself, without the Co-operation and Subjection of the Creature to Him in Humility. There God is an unmanifested God to the Creature. So the Angels dwell not with such a one; for wherever they dwell, there is the Glory of God; and they make His Glory. What then dwelleth in such a Creature as this? God dwelleth not therein; the Angels dwell not therein; God willeth not therein, the Angels also will not therein. The case is evidently this, in that Soul or Creature its OWN Will is without God's Will, and there the Devil dwelleth; and with him all whatever is without God, and without Christ. This is the Truth; lay it to Heart.

The Scholar:

It is possible I may ask several impertinent Questions; but I beseech you, good Sir, to have Patience with me, and to pity my Ignorance, if I ask what may appear to you perhaps ridiculous, or may not seem fit for me to expect an Answer to. For I have several Questions still to propound to you; but I am ashamed of my own Thoughts in this Matter.

The Master:

Be plain with me, and propose whatever is upon your Mind; yea, be not ashamed even to appear ridiculous, so that by Querying you may but become wiser.

The Scholar thanked his Master for this Liberty, and said:

How far then are Heaven and Hell asunder?

To whom he answered thus:

As far as Day and Night; or as far as Something and Nothing. They are in one another, and yet they are at the greatest Distance one from the other. Nay, the one of them is as nothing to the other; and yet notwithstanding they cause Joy and Grief to one another. Heaven is throughout the whole World, and It is also without the World over all, even everywhere that is, or that can be but so much as imagined. It filleth all; It is within all; It is without all; It encompasseth all; without Division, without Place; working by a Divine Manifestation, and flowing forth universally, but not going in the least out of Itself. For It worketh only in Itself, and is revealed, being ONE, and undivided in ALL. It appeareth only through the Manifestation of God; and never but in Itself only: And in that Being which cometh into It, or in that wherein It is manifested, there also it is that God is manifested. Because Heaven is nothing else but a Manifestation or Revelation of the Eternal ONE, wherein ALL the Working and Willing is in quiet LOVE.

So in like Manner Hell also is through the whole World, and dwelleth and worketh but in itself, and in that wherein the Foundation of Hell is manifested, namely, in SELF-hood, and in the False Will. The visible World hath both in it; and there is no Place but what Heaven and Hell may be found or revealed in it. Now Man as to his temporal Life, is only of the visible World; and therefore during the Time of this Life, he seeth not the spiritual World. For the outward World with its Substance, is a Cover to the spiritual World, even as the Body is to the Soul. But when the outward Man dieth, then the spiritual World, as to the Soul, which hath now its Covering taken away, is manifested either in the Eternal Light with the holy Angels, or in the Eternal Darkness, with the Devils.

The Scholar further queried:

What is an Angel, or a human Soul, that they can be thus manifested either in God's Love or Anger, either in Light or Darkness?

To whom Theophorus answered:

They come from one and the self-same Original: They are little Branches of the Divine Wisdom, of the Divine Will, sprung from the Divine Word, and made Objects of the Divine Love. They are out of the Ground of Eternity, whence Light and Darkness do spring: Darkness, which consisteth in the receiving of SELF-Desire: and Light, which consisteth in Willing the same Thing with God. For in the conformity of the Will with God's Will, is Heaven; and wheresoever there is this Willing with God, there the Love of God is undoubtedly in the Working, and His Light will not fail to manifest Itself. But in the SELF-Attraction of the Soul's Desire, or in the Reception of SELF into the Willing of any Spirit, Angelical or Human, the Will of God worketh difficultly, and is to that Soul or Spirit nought but Darkness; out of which, notwithstanding, the Light may be manifested. And this Darkness is the Hell of that Spirit wherein it is. For **Heaven** and **Hell** are nought else but a **Manifestation of the Divine Will either in Light or Darkness, according to the Properties of the Spiritual World**.

What the Body of Man is; and why the Soul is capable of receiving Good and Evil.

Scholar.

WHAT then is the Body of Man?

Master.

It is the visible World; an Image and Quintessence, or Compound of all that the World is; and the visible World is a Manifestation of the inward spiritual World, come out of the eternal Light, and out of the eternal Darkness, out of the spiritual Compaction or Connection; and it is also an Image or Figure of Eternity, whereby Eternity hath made itself visible; where SELF-Will and RESIGNED Will, viz. Evil and Good, work one with the other. Such a Substance is the outward Man. For God created Man of the outward World, and breathed into him the inward spiritual World for a Soul and intelligent Life; and therefore in the Things of the outward World, Man can receive and work Evil and Good.

Of the Destruction of the World; of Man's Body, in and after the Resurrection; where Heaven and Hell shall be; of the the Last Judgement; and wherefore the Strife in the Creature must be.

Scholar.

WHAT shall be after this World, when all Things perish and come to an End?

Master.

The material Substance only ceaseth; **viz.** the four

Elements, the Sun, Moon, and Stars. And then the inward World will be wholly visible and manifest. But whatsoever hath been wrought by the Will or Spirit of a Man in this World's Time, whether evil or good shall not cease. I say, every such Work shall there separate itself in a spiritual Manner, either into the Eternal Light, or into the Eternal Darkness. For that which is born from each Man's Will shall penetrateth and passeth again into that which is like itself. And there the Darkness is called Hell, and is an **eternal forgetting of all Good**; and the Light is called the Kingdom of God, and is an eternal Joy in and to the Saints, who continually glorify and praise God, for having delivered them from the Torment of Evil.

The Last Judgement is but a Kindling of the Fire both of God's Love and Anger, in which the Matter of every Substance perisheth, and each Fire shall attract into itself its own, that is, the Substance that is like itself: Thus God's Fire of Love will draw into It whatsoever is born in the Love of God, or Love-Principle, in which also It shall burn after the Manner of Love, and yield Itself into that Substance. But the Torment will draw into itself what is wrought in the Anger of God in Darkness, and consume the false Substance; and then there will remain only the painful aching Will in its own proper Nature, Image and Figure.

Scholar.

With what Matter and Form shall the human Body rise?

Master.

It is sown a natural gross and elementary Body, which in this Lifetime is like the outward Elements; yet in this gross Body there is a subtle Power and Virtue. As in the Earth also there is a subtle good Virtue, which is like the Sun, and is one and the same with the Sun; which also in the Beginning of Time did spring and proceed out of the Divine Power and Virtue, from whence all the good Virtue of the Body is likewise derived. This good Virtue of the mortal Body shall come again and live forever in a Kind of transparent crystalline material Property, in spiritual Flesh and Blood; as shall return also the good Virtue of the Earth, for the Earth likewise shall become crystalline, and the Divine Light shine in every Thing that hath a Being, Essence or Substance. And as the gross Earth shall perish and never return, so also the gross Flesh of Man shall perish and not live forever. But all Things must appear before the Judgement, and in the Judgement be separated by the Fire; yea, both the Earth, and also the Ashes of the human Body. For when God shall once move the spiritual World, every Spirit shall attract its spiritual Substance to itself. A good Spirit and Soul shall draw to itself its good Substance, and an evil one its evil Substance. But we must here understand by Substance, such a material Power and Virtue, the Essence of which is mere Virtue, like a material Tincture (such a Thing as hath all Figures, Colors, and Virtues in it, and is at the same Time transparent), the Grossness whereof shall have perished in all Things.

Scholar.

Shall we not rise again with our visible Bodies, and live in them forever?

Master.

When the visible World perisheth, then all that hath come out of it, and hath been external, shall perish with it. There shall remain of the World only the heavenly crystalline Nature and Form, and of Man also only the spiritual Earth; for Man shall be then wholly like the spiritual World, which as yet is hidden.

Scholar.

Shall there be Husband and Wife, or Children or Kindred, in the heavenly Life, or shall one associate with another, as they do in this Life?

Master.

Why art thou so fleshly-minded? There will be neither Husband nor Wife, but all will be like the Angels of God, Viz. Masculine Virgins. There will be neither Son nor Daughter, Brother nor Sister, but all of one Stock and Kindred. For all are but One in Christ, as a Tree and its Branches are one, though distinct as Creatures; but God is All in All. Indeed, there will be spiritual Knowledge of what every one hath been, and done, but no Possessing or Enjoying, or Desire of Possessing earthly Things, or Enjoying fleshly Relations any more.

Scholar.

Shall they all have that Eternal Joy and Glorification alike?

Master.

The Scripture saith, "**Such as the People is, such is their God**." And in another Place, "**With the holy thou art holy, and with the perverse thou art perverse**." And St.Paul saith, "**In the Resurrection one shall differ from another in Glory, as do the Sun, Moon, and Stars**." Therefore know, that the Blessed shall indeed all enjoy the Divine Working in and upon them; but their Virtue, and Illumination or Glory, shall be very different, according as they have been endued in this Life with different Measures and Degrees of Power and Virtue in their painful Working. For the painful Working of the Creature in this Lifetime is the opening and begetting of Divine Power, by which that Power is made movable and operative. Now those who have wrought with Christ in this Lifetime, and not in the Lust of the Flesh, shall have great Power and transcendent Glorification in and upon them. But others, who have only expected, and relied upon, an imputed Satisfaction, and in the meanwhile have served their Belly-God, and yet at last have turned, and obtained Grace; those, I say, shall not attain to so high a Degree of Power and Illumination. So that there will be as great a Difference of Degrees between them, as is between the Sun, Moon and Stars; or between the Flowers of the Field in their Varieties of Beauty, Power, and Virtue.

Scholar.

How shall the World be judged, and by Whom?

Master.

Jesus Christ, that "**Word of God which became Man**," shall by the Power of His Divine Stirring or Motion separate from Himself all that belongeth not to Him, and shall wholly manifest

His Kingdom in the Place or Space where this World now is; for the separating Motion worketh all over the Universe, through all at once.

Scholar.

Whither shall the Devils and all the Damned be thrown, when the Place of this World is become the Kingdom of Christ, and as Such shall be glorified? Shall they be cast out of the Place of this World? Or shall Christ have, and manifest His Dominion, out of the Sphere or Place of this World?

Master.

Hell shall remain in the Place or Sphere of this World everywhere, but hidden to the Kingdom of Heaven, as the Night is hidden in and to the Day. **"The Light shall shine forever in the Darkness, but the Darkness can never comprehend, or reach it**." And the Light is the Kingdom of Christ; but the Darkness is Hell, wherein the Devils and the Wicked dwell; and thus they shall be suppressed by the Kingdom of Christ, and made his Footstool, viz. a Reproach.

Scholar.

How shall all People and Nations be brought to Judgement?

Master.

The Eternal Word of God, out of which every spiritual creaturely Life hath proceeded, will move Itself at that Hour, according to Love and Anger, in every Life which is come out of the Eternity, and will draw every Creature before the Judgement of Christ, to be sentenced by this Motion of the World. The Life will then be manifested in all its Works, and every Soul shall see and feel its Judgement and Sentence in itself. For the Judgement is indeed immediately manifested in and to every Soul at the Departure of the Body; and the last Judgement is but a Return of the spiritual Body, and a Separation of the World, when the Evil shall be separated from the Good, in the substance of the World and of the human Body, and every Thing enters into its eternal Receptacle. And thus it is a Manifestation of the Mystery of God in every Substance and Life.

Scholar.

How will the Sentence be pronounced?

Master.

Here consider the Words of Christ. "**He will say to those on His Right-hand, Come, ye blessed of My Father, inherit the Kingdom prepared for you from the Foundation of the World. For I was hungry, and ye gave Me Meat; I was thirsty, and ye gave Me Drink; I was a Stranger, and ye took Me in; naked, and ye clothed Me. I was sick, and ye visited Me, in Prison, and ye came unto Me**". Then shall they answer Him, saying, "**Lord, when saw we Thee hungry, thirsty, a Stranger, naked, sick, or in Prison, and ministered thus unto Thee?**" And shall the King answer and say unto them; "**Inasmuch as ye have done it unto one of the least of these my Brethren, ye have done it unto Me.**" And unto the Wicked on His Left-hand He will say, "**Depart from Me, ye Cursed, into everlasting Fire, prepared for the Devil and his Angels. For I was hungry,** thirsty, a Stranger, naked, sick, and in Prison, and ye ministered not unto Me.**"** And they shall also answer Him and say, "**When did we see Thee thus, and ministered not unto Thee?**" And He will answer them, "**Verily I say unto you, inasmuch as ye have not done it unto one of the least of these, ye did it not to Me.**" **And these shall depart into everlasting Punishment, but the Righteous into Life Eternal**.

Scholar.

Loving Master, pray tell me why Christ saith, "**What you have done to the least of these, you have done to Me; and what you have not done to them, neither have you done it to Me.**" And how doth a Man in his Working, doeth it to **Christ Himself**?

Master.

Christ dwelleth really and essentially in the Faith of those that wholly yield up themselves to Him, and He giveth them His Flesh for Food, and His Blood for Drink; and thus He possesseth the Ground of their Faith, according to the interior or inward Man. And a True Christian is called a Branch of the Vine Christ, and a Christian, because Christ dwelleth spiritually in him; therefore whatsoever Good any shall do to such a Christian in his bodily Necessities, it is done to Christ Himself, Who dwelleth in him. For such a Christian is not his own, but is wholly resigned to Christ, and become His peculiar Possession, and consequently the good Deed is done to Christ **Himself**.

Therefore also, whosoever shall withhold their Help from such a needy Christian, and forbear to serve him in his Necessity, they thrust Christ away from themselves, and despise Him in His Members. When a poor Person that belongeth thus to Christ, asketh any Thing of thee, and thou deniest it him in his Necessity, thou deniest it to Christ Himself. And whatsoever hurt any shall do to such a Christian, they do it to Christ Himself. When any mock, scorn, revile, reject, or thrust away such a one, they do all that to Christ; but he that receiveth him, giveth him Meat and Drink, or Apparel, and assisteth him in his necessities, doth it likewise to Christ, and to a Fellow-Member of his own Body. Nay he even doth it to himself, if he be a True Christian; for we are all One in Christ, as a Tree and its Branches are.

Scholar.

How then will those subsist in the Day of that fierce Judgement, who afflict and vex the poor and distressed, and deprive them of their very Sweat; necessitating and constraining them by Force to submit to their Wills, and trampling upon them as their Footstools, only that they themselves may live in Pomp and Power, and spend the Fruits of this poor People's Sweat and Labor in Voluptuousness, Pride, and Vanity?

Master.

Christ suffereth in the Persecution of His Members. Therefore all the Wrong that such hard Exactors do to the poor Wretches under their Control, is done to Christ Himself; and falleth under His severe Sentence and Judgement! And besides that, they help the Devil to augment his Kingdom; for by such

Oppression of the Poor they draw them off from Christ, and make them seek unlawful Ways to fill their Bellies. Nay, they work for, and with the Devil himself, doing the very same Thing which he doth; who, without Intermission, opposeth the Kingdom of Christ, which consisteth only in Love. All these Oppressors, if they do not turn with their whole Hearts to Christ, and minister to, or serve Him, must go into Hell-Fire, which is fed and kept alive by nothing else but such mere SELF, as that which they have exercised over the Poor here.

Scholar.

But how will it fare with those, and how will they be able to stand that severe Trial, who in this Time do so fiercely contend about the Kingdom of Christ, and slander, revile, and persecute one another for their Religion, as they do?

Master.

All such have not yet known Christ; and they are but as a Type or Figure of Heaven and Hell, striving with each other for the Victory.

All rising, swelling Pride, which contendeth about Opinions, is an Image of SELF. And whosoever hath not Faith and Humility, nor liveth in the Spirit of Christ, which is Love, is only armed with the Anger of God, and helpeth forward the Victory of the imaginary SELF, that is, the Kingdom of Darkness, and the Anger of God. For at the Day of Judgement all SELF shall be given to the Darkness, as shall also all the unprofitable Contentions of Men; in which they seek not after Love, but merely after their imaginary SELF, that they may exalt themselves by exalting and establishing their OWN Opinions; even stirring up Princes to Wars for the Sake of the same, and by that Means occasioning the Desolation of whole Countries of People. All such Things belong to the Judgement, which will separate the False from the True; and then all Images or Opinions shall cease, and all the Children of God shall dwell forever in the Love of Christ, and That in them.

All whosoever in this Time of Strife, namely, from the Fall to the Resurrection, are not zealous in the Spirit of Christ, and desirous to promote Peace and

Love, but seek and strive for themSELVES only, are of the Devil, and belong to the Pit of Darkness, and must consequently be separated from Christ. For in Heaven all serve God their Creator in Humble Love.

Scholar.

Wherefore then doth God suffer such Strife and Contention to be in this Time?

Master.

The Life itself standeth in Strife, that it may be made manifest, sensible, and palpable, and that the Wisdom may be made separable and known.

The Strife also constituteth the eternal Joy of the Victory. For there will arise great Praise and Thanksgiving in the Saints from the experimental Sense and Knowledge that Christ in them hath overcome Darkness, and all the SELF of Nature, and that they are at length totally delivered from the Strife; at which they shall rejoice eternally, when they shall know how the Wicked are recompensed. And therefore God suffereth all Souls to stand in the Free-Will, that the eternal Dominion both of Love and Anger, of Light and Darkness, may be made manifest and known; and that every Life might cause and find its own Sentence in itself. For that which is now a Strife and Pain to the Saints in their wretched Warfare here, shall in the End be turned into great Joy to them; and that which hath been a Joy and Pleasure to ungodly Persons in this World, shall afterwards be turned into eternal Torment and Shame to them. Therefore the Joy of the Saints must arise to them out of Death, as the Light ariseth out of a Candle by the Destruction and Consumption of it in its Fire; that so the Life may be freed from the Painfulness of Nature, and possess another World.

And as the Light hath quite another Property than the Fire hath, for It giveth and yieldeth Itself forth; whereas the Fire draweth in and consumeth itself; so the holy Life of Meekness springeth forth through the Death of SELF-Will, and then God's Will of Love only ruleth, and doth ALL in ALL. For thus the Eternal ONE hath attained Feeling and

Separability, and brought Itself forth again with the Feeling, through Death in great Joyfulness; that there might be an Eternal Delight in the Infinite Unity, and an Eternal Cause of Joy; and therefore that which was before Painfulness, must now be the Ground and cause of this Motion or stirring to the Manifestation of all Things. And herein lieth the Mystery of the hidden Wisdom of God.

Every one that asketh receiveth, every one that seeketh findeth; and to every one that knocketh it shall be opened. The Grace of our Lord Jesus Christ, and the Love of God, and the Communion of the Holy Ghost, be with us all.

Amen.

THE LIFE OF JACOB BEHMEN

THE TEUTONIC THEOSOPHER

*W*hoever have made their Appearance in the World in a truly godlike Form, and only in a pure spiritual Ministration, it has had the greatest Antipathy, and Aversion to them that can possibly be conceived. And in the whole Creation, there are not two Forms of Beings more intirely contrary to each other.

It is very true, that *Moses, Joshua, Samuel, David,* and Others, came forth in this Life in much Applause, but had withal a Delegation to the temporal Magistracy, wherein by God's good Power they led the People through many Difficulties, made them victorious, and gave them Possessions, and Reputation among the Nations round them; all which allayed and lessened the Hatred, which the divine Form in which they lived necessarily produces.

And yet, notwithstanding, some of them had died under the People's Hands, had not God entrusted with them, upon desperate Mutinies, miraculous Operations, beyond the Power of ordinary Men, to put a stop to the heady Rage of the Multitude.

But as for those, whom in these last Ages he has sent with this plain uncouth Message to Mankind, to injoin them to strive with Earnestness, telling them they shall have Heaven, a Joy, a Paradise, a Territory, a Dominion; but that all this is in themselves; the Territory is themselves; that it is in the Devil's Possession; there he rules, and lives; that with him they must encounter, and cast him forth, else their expected Heaven will turn into a Hell; these are dismal Messengers of odious Things, especially to those, that in their several Forms of Religion have been promised eternal Happiness at a far cheaper Rate.

We may appeal to the World, whether these Messengers of evil Tidings do not well deserve to be crucified, and the Doctrines of INDULGENCE and IMPUTATION restored to their ancient Dignity.

There is a small Market-Town in the *Upper Lusatia*, called *Old Seidenburg*, distant from *Gorlitz* about a Mile and half, in which lived a Man whose Name was *Jacob*, and his Wife's Name was *Ursula*. People they were of the poorest Sort, yet of sober and honest Behaviour. In the Year 1575 they had a Son, whom they names *Jacob*. This was the divinely-illuminated JACOB BEHMEN, the *Teutonic Theosopher*, whom God raised up, in the most proper Period, both as to the Chiliad and Century, to show the Ground of the Mystery of Nature and Grace, and open the Wonders of his Wisdom. His Education was suitable to their Wealth, his first Employment being the Care of the common Cattle among the rest of the Youths of the Town. But when grown older, he was placed at School, where he learnt to read and write, and was from thence put Apprentice to a Shoemaker in *Gorlitz*. Having served his Time, in the year 1594 he took to Wife *Catharine*, the Daughter of *John Hunshman*, a Citizen of *Gorlitz*, and had by her four Sons, living in the State of Matrimony thirty Years: His Sons he placed in his Life-time to several honest Trades. He fell sick in *Silesia* of a hot burning Ague, contracted by too much drinking of Water, and was at his Desire brought to *Gorlitz*, and died there in 1624, being near fifty years of Age, and was buried in the Church yard.

As in Men that have appeared to the World with great and superior Accomplishments, to promote some great Design beyond the POWERS of Nature, it has pleased God to usher them in with some signal Dispensations, to direct the Eye of the World to observe his Work; so in this Instance of *Jacob Behmen*, not only a new Star mystically appeared some Time before his Birth, but when he was a Herd's Boy he had a most remarkable Trial, and providential Preservation and Prevention. For in the Heat of Mid-Day, retiring from his Playfellows to a little stony Crag just by, called the *Lands Crown*, where the natural Situation of the Rock had made a seeming Inclosure of some Part of the Mountain; finding an Entrance, he went in, and saw there a large wooden Vessel full of Money, at which Sight, being in a sudden Astonishment, he in Haste retired, not moving his Hand to it, and came and related his Fortune to the rest of the Boys, who coming with him, sought often and with much Diligence an Entrance, but could not find any. But some Years after, a foreign Artist, as *Jacob Behmen* himself related, skilled in finding out magical Treasures, took it away, and thereby much enriched himself, yet perished by an infamous Death, that Treasure being lodged there, and covered with a Curse to him that should find and take it away.

Truly, this appears to have been a Seduction of this tender Youth into this Cave of *Pluto*, and to have had a destructive Design in it. Our Saviour had the World and the Glory of it offered to Himself, but the Condition was intolerable.

When he had been for a Time an Apprentice, his Master and his Mistress being abroad, there came a Stranger to the Shop, of a reverend and grave Countenance, yet in mean Apparel, and taking up a Pair of Shoes, desired to buy them. The Boy, being scarce got higher than sweeping the Shop, would not presume to set a Price on them, but told him his Master and Mistress were not at Home, and himself durst not venture the Sale of any Thing without their Order.

But the Stranger being very importunate, he offered them at a Price, which if he got, he was certain would save him harmless in parting from them, supposing also thereby to be rid of the importunate Chapman {peddler or merchant}. But the old Man paid down the Money, took the Shoes, and departed from the Shop a little Way, where standing still, with a loud and an earnest Voice, he called, *Jacob, Jacob, come forth.* The Boy, within hearing of the Voice, came out in a great Fright, at first amazed at the Stranger's familiar calling him by his Christian Name, but recollecting himself, he went to him. The Man with a severe but friendly Countenance, fixing his Eyes upon him (which were bright and sparkling) took him by his right Hand, and said to him:

Jacob, *thou art little, but shalt be great, and become another Man, such a one as at whom the World shall wonder. Therefore be pious, fear God, and reverence his Word. Read diligently the Holy Scriptures, wherein you have Comfort and Instruction. For thou must endure much Misery and Poverty, and suffer Persecution, but be courageous and persevere, for God loves, and is gracious to thee.* And therewith pressing his Hand, he looked with a bright sparkling Eye fixed on his Face, and departed.

This Prediction took deep Impression on *Jacob*'s Mind, and made him bethink himself, and grow serious in his Actions, keeping his Thoughts stirring in Consideration of the Caution he had received from that Man.

So that from thenceforward he much more frequented the public Worship, and profited well therein in the outward Reformation of his Life; seriously considering with himself that Speech of our Saviour, *Luke 11,13. My Father which is in Heaven will give the Spirit to him that asks him,* he was thereby thoroughly awakened in himself, and set forward to desire that promised Comforter; and continuing in that Earnestness, he was at last, in his own Expression, *surrounded with a divine Light for seven Days, and stood in the highest Contemplation and Kingdom of Joys.* And this happened to him, whilst he was with his Master in the Country about the Affairs of his Vocation.

When the Vision and Revelation were passed by him, he grew more and more accurately attentive to his Duty to God and Neighbour, diligently frequented the Church, read the Scriptures, and lived in all Observance of outward Ministrations. Scurrilous and blasphemous Words he would rebuke, even in his own Master, who was somewhat intemperate in his Tongue; and from Day to Day continuing upon his Watch, he endeavoured after the Christian Growth, becoming, by his Contrariety of Manners, a Scorn and Derision to the World. And at last his own Master, being not able to bear a Reprover so near Home in that Relation, set him at

Liberty, with full Permission to seek his Livelihood as he liked best.

After this, about the Year 1600, in the twenty fifth Year of his Age, he was again surrounded by the divine Light, and replenished with the heavenly Knowledge; insomuch, as going abroad into the Fields, to a Green before *Neys-Gate*, at *Gorlitz*, he there sat down, and viewing the Herbs and Grass of the Field, in his inward Light he saw into their Essences, Use and Properties, which were discovered to him by their Lineaments, Figures, and Signatures.

In like Manner he beheld the whole Creation, and from that Fountain of Revelation he afterwards wrote his Book, *De Signatura Rerum*. In the unfolding of those Mysteries before his Understanding, he had a great Measure of Joy, yet returned Home and took Care of his Family, and lived in great Peace and Silence, scarce intimating to any these wonderful Things that had befallen him, till in the Year 1610, being again taken into this Light, lest the Mysteries revealed to him should pass through him as a Stream, and rather for a Memorial, than intending any Publication, he wrote his first Book, called *Aurora*, or *The Morning-Redness*.

The Book being found about him by a Man of great Quality, with whom he conversed, was received with that Desire, that he immediately disjoined it, and caused it to be copied out in a few Hours.

Thus, contrary to the Author's Intention, it became public, and after a while, fell into the Hands of *Gregory Ricter,* the Superintendent of *Gorlitz,* who making Use of his Pulpit, and the Liberty he had of speaking without an Opposer, to revile what and whom he pleased, he endeavoured to stir up the Magistracy, to exercise their Jurisdiction in rooting out this supposed Church-Weed.

And this he did with so much Vehemence, and Pretence of godly Zeal, that the Senate took some Notice of it, and convened *Jacob Behmen* before them, seizing his Book, and admonishing him to employ his Mind in the Affairs of his Trade, and for the Future leave off writing any more Books, which he saw gave so much Offence.

This Occasion brought this Man first into public Notice, for at the Hearing of the Business, such was the unchristian Heat and Violence of the Minister, and so much the Meekness of *Jacob Behemen*, that it gave great Advantage to his Reputation, and Credit to that inward School, from whence he came out so well taught.

This very Book, which the Senate had seized on, was by themselves afterwards presented to the Prince Elector of *Saxony*'s Marshall of his House, *George Pflugen*, in 1641, when he came to *Gorlitz*, being brought to Light by D.P.S a Burgomaster of *Gorlitz*; and it was sent by the Marshal to *Amsterdam*, where it was printed.

Upon the Command of the Senate, he refrained from writing seven Years; at the End of which, a new Motion from on high seizing on him, and taking captive these rational human Prohibitions, he wrote again; out of what Principle, and how moved, his own Words can best express.

"Art, *says he*, has not wrote here, neither was there any Time to consider how to set punctually down, according to the right Understanding of the Letters, but all was ordered according to the Direction of the Spirit, which often went in Haste; so that in many Words, Letters may be wanting, and in some Places a Capital Letter for a Word; so that the Penman's Hand, by reason he was not accustomed to it, did often shake. And though I could have wrote in a more accurate, fair, and plain Manner, yet the Reason was this, that the burning Fire often forced forward with Speed, and the Hand and Pen must hasten directly after it; for *it comes and goes as a sudden Shower.*" And further he says, "I can write nothing of myself, but as a Child which neither knows nor understands any Thing, which neither has ever been learnt, but only that which the Lord vouchsafes to know in me, according to the Measure as himself manifests in me.

"For I never desired to know any Thing of the Divine Mystery, much less understood I the Way to seek and find it. I knew nothing of it, as it is the Condition of poor Laymen in their Simplicity.

"I sought only after the Heart of Jesus Christ, that I might hide myself therein from the wrathful Anger of God, and the violent Assaults of the Devil. And I besought the Lord earnestly for his Holy Spirit and his Grace, that he would please to bless and guide me in him, and take that away from me which turned me from him; and I resigned myself wholly to him, that I might not live to my own Will but his; and that he only might lead and direct me, to the End I might be his Child in his Son Jesus.

"In this my earnest and Christian Seeking and Desire (wherein I suffered many a shrewd Repulse, but at last resolved rather to put myself in Hazard, than give over and leave off) the Gate was opened to me, that in one Quarter of an Hour I saw and knew more, than if I had been many Years together at an University, at which I exceedingly admired, and thereupon turned my Praise to God for it.

"For I saw and knew the Being of all Beings, the Byss and the Abyss, and the eternal Generation of the *Holy Trinity*, the Descent and Original of the World, and of all Creatures through the Divine Wisdom: I knew and saw in myself all the three Worlds, namely, *The Divine*, angelical, and paradisical; and *The Dark World*, the Original of the Nature to the Fire; and then, thirdly, the *external* and *visible World*, being a Procreation or external Birth from both the internal and spiritual Worlds. And I saw and knew the whole working Essence, in the Evil and the Good, and the Original and Existence of each of them; and likewise how the fruitful-bearing Womb of Eternity brought forth.

"So that I did not only greatly wonder at it, but did also exceedingly rejoice, and presently it came powerfully into by Mind to set the same down in Writing, for a Memorial for myself, though I could very hardly apprehend the same, in my external Man, and express it with the Pen.

"Yet however I must begin to labour in these great Mysteries, as a Child that goes to School. I saw it as in a great Deep in the Internal.

"For I had a thorough View of the Universe, as in a Chaos, wherein all Things are couched and wrapped up, but it was impossible for me to explain the same.

"Yet it opened itself in me, from Time to Time, as in a young Plant; though the same was with me for the Space of twelve Years, and it was as it were breeding, and I found a powerful Instigation within me, before I could bring it forth into external Form of Writing; and whatever I could apprehend with the external Principle of my Mind, that I wrote down.

"But however afterwards the Sun shone upon me a good While, but not constantly, for the Sun hid itself, and then I knew not, nor well understood by own Labour. So that Man must acknowledge, that his Knowledge is not his own, but from God, who manifests the *Ideas* of Wisdom to the Soul of Man, in what Measure he pleases." See further relating to this Point, what is contained in this Volume. *Aurora,* Chap.19. ver. 4–16. Chap. 25. ver. 4–10. Chap. 11. ver. 135, 136. Chap. 12. ver. 146–151. Chap. 14. ver. 55–58. Chap. 18. ver. 93. Chap. 21. ver. 69–71. Chap. 22. ver. 38. *The Three Principles,* Chap. 10. ver. 1. Chap. 24. ver. 16. Chap. 2. ver. 4–6. Chap. 22. ver. 50. Many other Places might be referred to in his Writings, but these are sufficient.

In this Light, and from this Principle, he wrote his Books, a Catalogue of which is at the End of the Life.

His Persecution, which was begun by the "Primate of *Gorlitz,* his principal Persecutor, is thus related.

This Minister had lent a young Baker a Dollar, to buy a little Meal, to make Cakes against the Holidays, out of which he brought him a pretty large One for a Thank-offering. And having within a Fortnight sold off his Batch, he restores him presently his Money with Thanks, not imagining an Expectation of any further Intereset for so short a Loan. But this it seems satisfied him not; the Minister in high Rage curses the Man, with little less than Damnation to his Soul; upon which he, despairing of his Salvation, falls into a deep Melancholy, and being almost distracted, his Wife gets her

Kinsman, *Jacob Behmen*, to come and confer with him; who having heard the Cause of his Distemper, and comforted him, repairs to the angry Clergyman, expresses with all Submission the young Man's Error, if he had through Ignorance of his Pleasure committed any, offers him, if he desired it, the utmost Satisfaction, and upon these Terms intreats his Favour to the perplexed Soul.

But the Minister turning his Choler upon the Intercessor, demands angrily, What had he to do to trouble him? And bids him get him gone about his own Business, or he would send him away with a Vengeance. So seeing no Hopes of appeasing him, he prays to God to keep his Worship, and was going to depart; but before he was got out of the Door, the furious Prelate enraged yet more at his mild Salutation, throws his Slipper at him, calling him wicked Rascal, disdaining a good Night from his Mouth. The humble Man, nothing moved at it, takes up the Slipper, and lays it at his Feet, intreats him not to be angry, says that he knew not how he had wronged him, prays God to have him in his keeping, and so departs.

The Superintendent's Choler does not yet cease boiling; the next *Sunday* he rails bitterly in the Pulpit against *Jacob Behmen*, even by Name, thunders against the Senate for tolerating such a pernicious Heretic, and sworn Enemy of the ministerial Function, who not content to write blasphemous Books, and pervert Souls, durst presume to come and disturb the Minister in his own House; and tells them, that if they longer suffered, and did not expel him their Territories, they would move God in his Wrath to sink their City, as he did those Withstanders of *Moses* and *Aaron*, the rebellious *Korah*, *Dathan*, and *Abiram*, with their Accomplices.

The innocent Man, all the While he was thus bitterly railed against, sat just at a Pillar directly over-against the Pulpit, heard all with Patience, and staid in the Church till all were gone out, and the Superintendent among the last; he followed him into the Church-yard, and there told him he was grieved to hear himself so publickly, and as he thought without Cause, defamed, yet requested, that rather than proceed in that Way of public Reproach, he would know his Offence, and it should be amended. The Minister at first would give no Answer to his Suit; at length, upon much Importunity, turning to him with a fell and stern Visage, he cries, Get thee behind me Satan! avant, thou turbulent unquiet Spirit, to thy Abyss of Hell!

Dost thou still persist, without all Respect to my Function, to molest and disgrace me? To which surly Repulse, the true-spirited Christian gave this incomparable modest Reply.

Yea, Reverend Sir, I know well, and much honour your Function. I desire not to fix any Aspersion upon it, or yourself, only intreat you, for your own and your Function's Honour, which engages you not to trample upon a submissive Offender, much less one that is innocent, to tell me candidly where my Fault lies. And further, turning to the Chaplain, said; Reverend and courteous Sir, I pray be pleased to intercede for me with our Minister, that he would, laying aside this violent Passion, tell me ingenuously wherein I have offended him, that I may, by the best Satisfaction I can, appease his Wrath, and he may cease incensing the Magistrate against me. But no Submission would allay his Rage, but in Heat he sends his Servant for the Town-Serjeant to lay hold of him, and carry him away to Prison: But his Chaplain, modestly excusing the poor Man, dissuaded him from the Execution of this Part of his Fury.

The next Morning, the Senators meeting in the Council-house, cited *Jacob Behmen* to appear before them, and examined him of his Life, and the Scandal he had given the Minister, that made him with such Vehemence exclaim against him. But he constantly affirming he was entirely ignorant of any just Cause of Offence he had given him, and humbly praying he might be sent for, to declare the Grounds of his Accusation, they esteeming this a just Motion, sent two Men of Quality of the Town to him, to desire him either to come and personally make known his Grievances to the Court, or at least inform them of the Matter, by those they had sent to him for that Purpose. But he again falling into a Passion at this Demand, said, he had nothing to do with the Council-house; what he had to say he would speak in his Council-throne, the Pulpit; what he there dictated they must obey without Contradiction, and without more ado, disable this wicked Heretic from further opposing the ministerial Function, by banishing him from their City; else the Curse of *Korah, Dathan,* and *Abiram,* would light upon them all.

Upon this the poor Senate, a little terrified, fearing the Preacher's Spleen, and his Power in the Duke of *Saxony*'s Court, fell to fresh Consultation; and some of the more upright and moderate Men (seeing neither their Reasons nor Votes able to countervail the Fears or worse Passions of the major Part) departing the Court, the rest, upon this mere groundless Clamour of their *Caiaphas*, hastily passed a Sentence of Banishment against their innocent Fellow-Citizen, and prosecuted it with all Vehemence. He hearing it, said only, Gentlemen, with all willing Submission I obey your Decree, only desire I may go Home to my House to settle my small Affairs there, and take my Family along with me, or at least take Leave of them; but neither would this small Piece of Humanity be allowed him, but he must, according to the Court's unalterable Decree, forthwith depart. His Answer was, That seeing it would be no better, he was content, and thereupon presently went out of Town, spending the Remainder of the Day in a melancholy Walk about the Town-fields, and the Night in what Harbour we know not.

But the Senate, meeting again next Morning, upon more sober Thoughts repealed their Sentence, and sent to seek out their innocent Exile, and brought him back with Honour: Yet still tired with the Prelate's incessant Clamour, they at length sent for him again, and intreated him, that in Love to the City's Quiet, he would seek himself a habitation elsewhere; which if he would please to do, they should hold themselves obliged to him for it, as an acceptable Service. In Compliance with this friendly Request of theirs, he removed from thence.

After this, upon a Citation, *Jacob Behmen* came to *Dresden*, before his Highness the Prince Elector of *Saxony*, where were assembled six Doctors of Divinity, Dr. *Hoe*, Dr. *Meisner*, Dr. *Baldwin*, Dr. *Gerhard*, Dr. *Leysern*, and another Doctor, and two Professors of the Mathematics. And these, in the Presence of his Highness the Prince Elector, begun to examine him concerning his Writings, and the high Mysteries therein; and many profound Queries in Divinity, Philosophy, and the Mathematics, they proposed to him. To all which he replied with such Meekness of Spirit, such Depth of Knowledge, and Fulness of Matter, that none of those Doctors and Professors returned one Word of Dislike or Contradiction.

The Prince his Highness much admired him, and required to know the Result of their Judgments, in what they had heard. But the Doctors and Examiners desired to be excused, and intreated his Highness that he would have Patience, till the Spirit of the Man had more plainly declared itself, for in many Particulars they could not understand him. Nevertheless they hoped, that hereafter he would make it more clear to them, and then they would offer their Judgments, but for the present they could not.

Then *Jacob Behmen* proposed some Questions to them, to which they returned Answers with much Modesty, and as it were amazed that they should (so much beyond their Expectation) hear from a Man of that mean Quality and Education, such mysterious Depths as were beyond the Reach of their Comprehension.

Then he conferred with them touching most of the Errors of those Times; pointing as it were with the Finger at the Original of them severally, declaring to them the naked Truth, and the great Difference betwixt that and some erroneous Suppositions.

To the *Astrologers* also, having discoursed something of their Science, he said, *Behold, thus far is the Knowledge of your Art right and good, grounded in the Mystery of Nature; but what is over and above* (instancing in several Particulars) *are mere heathenish Additions, the Folly and Blindness of Heathens, which we Christian ought not to follow or imitate.*

Then his Highness the Prince Elector, being very much satisfied with his Answers, took him apart from the Company, and discoursed with him a good Space concerning several Points of Difficulty, wherein being well satisfied, he courteously dismissed him.

After this Examination, Dr. *Meisner,* and Dr. *Gerhard,* meeting at *Wittenberg,* begun to discourse of *Jacob Behmen,* expressing how greatly they admired the continued Harmony of Scriptures produced by him at his Examination, and that they would not, for all the World, have served his Enemies Malice in censuring him; *For,* says Dr. *Meisner, who knows but God may have designed him for some extraordinary Work, and how can we with Justice pass Judgment against that we understand not? For surely he seems to be a Man of wonderful high Gifts of the Spirit, though we cannot at present, from any Ground of Certainty, approve or disapprove of many Things he holds!*

How much more ingenuous is this, than the Character given him by *Jo. Laur. Moshemius,* Chancellor of the University of *Gottingen,* and ecclesiatic Historian, quoted by the Bishop of *Gloucester,* Dr. *Warburton?* "JAC. BÖHMIUS, *Sutor Görlicensis, Vir innumeris & Amicis & Inimicis inclytus, quem Theosophum Germanicum Patroni salutant. Hic cum Natura ipsa proclivis esset ad Res abditas pervestigandas, & Rob. Fluddii ac Rosacrucianorum*

Scita cognovisset, Thelogiam, Igne Duce, Imaginatione Comite invenit, ipsis Pythagoricis Numeris & Heracliti Notis obscuriorem,—ita enim Chymicis Imaginationibus & tanta Verborum Confusione & Caligine omnia miscet, ut ipse fibi obserepere videatur. " By this he would insinuate, directly contrary to what has been shown, that he derived his Knowledge from Chemistry and chemical Writers; or as he says in another Place, that he owed his whole Wisdom to one of them he there specifies. What Credit can be given to an Historian in Matters more remote, when he has given so unfair an Account in what is so well known? A fit Historian for such a Divine, as is capable of characterizing that *great Light of the Age*, Mr. *Law*, as the Bishop has done. "*When I reflect on his wonderful Infatuation, who has spent a Long Life in hunting after, and with an incredible Appetite devouring, the Trash dropt from every Species of Mysticism, it puts me in Mind of what Travellers tell us of a horrid Fanaticism in the East, where the Devotee makes a solemn Vow never to taste of other Food than what has passed through the Entrails of some impure or savage Animal. Hence their whole Lives are passed (like Mr.* Law's *among his Ascetics) in Woods and Forests, far removed from the Converse of Mankind.* " This Passage fully shows the State of Mind of the Writer of it, and no

Censure passed upon it can add to it. See, in this Volume, *The Three Principles*, Chap.3 ver. 6—8. Chap.25. ver. 29, 30. Chap 8. Ver.15. How different from these was the Son of the Primate of *Gorlitz?* His Father, who had been so violent a Persecutor of *Jacob Behmen* had in the most ignominious Manner wrote against him; to which the blessed Man so well replied, that he totally silenced him. After the Decease of both, willing to consult the Honour of his Father, he determined to write an Answer, that he might remove the Odium from him. But behold a most unexpected Event! Reading *Jacob Behmen*'s Writings, to finish the Design he had in View, his Mind is convinced, and affected in such a Manner, that instead of proceeding in his former Purpose, he was rather disposed to take up his Pen in Defence of our Author, crying out, with Astonishment, in this mournful Exclamation, " *Oh! my Father, what hast thou done?*" So great was the Power of Truth on his Mind.

It was the *Pharisees* Judgment of our Saviour, *Say we not well thou art a Samaritan, and hast a Devil?* And in another Place, *This Man casts out Devils by Beelzebub the Prince of Devils.* So unwilling is human Reason to submit, or conceive a Possibility of that perfect Wisdom and Power, that in Death and Self-denial is brought forth to the Glory of him, that is the Father of it.

The same Measure *Jacob Behmen* received in his Generation. For the Appearance of that unusual Knowledge and deep Revelation of Mysteries, in a Vessel so contemptible to the magnificent Mind of Man, brought such hard Censures as these from the stupid World, which appeared One Time more especially. The Manner was thus.

Sitting by himself in his House, a Man knocked at his Door, to which repairing, a Person of a mean Stature, of a sharp and stern Look, saluted him courteously, congratulating him on that great and wonderful Knowledge he had received, and humbly let him know, that he heard that he was blest with a singular Spirit, the like to which had not lately appeared among the Children of Men; that it was a humane and friendly Duty, incumbent upon every Man to impart the good Things vouchsafed him to his needy Neighbour, and himself was now a needy Petitioner, that he would yield some of the Spirit to him. In which Request if he pleased to gratify him, he would, in such Things wherein he abounded, give a suitable Recompence, making a covert Offer of some Monies, to satisfy *Jacob Behmen*'s Necessities.

To whom he replied, with Thanks, *That he accounted himself unworthy of the Esteem of having these greater Gifts and Arts, as was by him imagined, and found only in himself an intire Love to his Neighbour, and simple Perseverance in the upright Belief and Faith in God; and for any other Endowments beyond these, he neither had them, nor esteemed them; much less* (as his Word seemed to intimate) *enjoyed the Society of any familiar Spirit.*

But, says he, *if there be in you that Desire of obtaining the Spirit of God, you must, as I have done, enter into earnest Repentance, and pray the Father, from whom all good Gifts proceed, and he will give it, and it will lead you into all Truth.*

This foolish Man, contemning this plain Instruction, became uncivilly importunate, and begun with Words of Magic Conjuration, to force the supposed familiar Spirit from *Jacob Behmen.*

At which Boldness and Folly, *Jacob Behmen*, being not a little moved in Spirit, took him by the Right-hand, and looked him sternly in the Face, intending an Imprecation to his perverse Soul. At which this Exorcist, trembling and amazed, asked Forgiveness; whereupon *Jacob Behmen* remitted his Zeal, dehorting {dissuading} him earnestly from that simonian and diabolical Practice, and permitted him, in Hopes of future Amendment, to depart in Peace.

The Publication of his first Book, the *Aurora*, or *Morning-Redness*, brought from all Parts great Resort to him of learned Men, and more especially of Chemists; with whom conversing much, he got the Use of those *Latin* and *Greek* Words that are frequent in his Works, as being significant Expression of those Notions that were in his Mind, and of great use and Convenience, for the illustration of what he had to propose.

Of those learned Men, that conversed with him in the greatest Familiarity was one *Balthazar Walter*; this Gentleman was a *Silesian* by Birth, by Profession a Physician, and had, in the Search of the ancient Magic Learning, travelled through *Egypt, Syria,* and *Arabia*, and found there such small Remains of it, that he returned unsuccessful and unsatisfied unto his own Country; where hearing of this Man, he repaired to him, and did, as the Queen of *Sheba* with King *Solomon*, try him with those hard Questions concerning the Soul, which, with the Answers to them, are now public in many Languages. From whence, and from frequent Discourses with him, he was so satisfied, that he stayed there three Months, and professed, that from his Conversation he had received more solid Answers to his curious Scruples, than he had found among the best Wits of those more promising Climates: And for the Future, he desisted from following Rivulets, since God had opened a Fountain at his own Door.

After his Examination at *Dresden*, and the Publication of his Book, it pleased God to turn the Hearts of many learned Men and Preachers, to the studying themselves, and teaching others those Doctrines of the Regeneration, and the Means of attaining it, they had formerly in a blind Zeal exclaimed against as Heretical; whereupon they ceased from preaching up Disputes and Controversies in Religion, as prejudicial to divine Charity, and the common Peace of Mankind; but for the Solution of all Doubts, they referred Men to an earnest Endeavour after the Recovery of the Life of Christ, the only Fountain of all true Light, and right Understanding in divine Things.

Thus was that excellent Light, shining in this heavenly Man's Soul, by the cross Design of a malicious Adversary, set in its Candlestick, and brought to open View, to give Light to the World. So that his Writings came to read in *Russia, Sweden, Poland,*

Denmark, the *Netherlands, England, Germany, France, Spain, Italy,* and even in the City of *Rome.* For by these Examinations, the Man's Worth came to be taken Notice of, and his Writings sought for and studied, not only by mean People, but by many great Rabbies of the Church, and Great Men of the World. Nay, Many in their Hearts Infidels to all Religion, in catching only at the Bait of his mysterious Philosophy, were drawn to the true Faith and Church of God.

Let us with Oil in our Lamps, and the Wedding Garment of a renewed Spirit, prepare to meet the Lord at his Coming.

His Superscription, and Motto, in all his Letters, were these Words; *Our Salvation in the Life of Jesus Christ in us.*

In his Seal-ring he had engraven a Hand stretched out from Heaven, with a Twig of three blown Lilies.

It has been a Custom with many in *Germany*, to carry a little Paper Book in their Pockets, into which their Friends write some remarkable Sentence, and subscribe their Names, and this Book is called *Album Amicorum,* [The Book of Friendship.] Into such as these our Author wrote these Verses:

To whom Time and Eternity Harmoniously as One agree; His Soul is safe, his Life's amended, His Battle's o'er, his Strife is ended.
Or thus, *Whose Time and Ever are all one, His Soul's at rest, his Warfare's done.*

When the Hour of his Departure was at hand, he called his Son *Tobias,* and asked him, Whether he heard that sweet harmonious Musick? He replied, No. Open, says he, the Door, that you may the better hear it. And asking what o'Clock it was, he told him it was Two: My Time, says he, in not yet, three Hours hence is my time: In the mean While he spoke these Words, *O thou strong God of Zebaoth, deliver me according to thy Will. Thou crucified Lord Jesus have Mercy on me, and take me into thy Kingdom.*

When Six in the Morning came, he took Leave of his Wife and Son, blessed them, and said, *Now I go hence into Paradise.* And bidding his Son turn him, he fetched a deep Sigh and departed.

Thus have you seen the Journey of this blessed Man on Earth, with his last Farewell. Over his Grave was erected the following Device, as sent from a Friend of his out of *Silesia:* A black wooden Cross, with the *Hebrew* Name *JHSVH* and twelve golden Beams encompassing it, under which rested a Child on a Death's Head, with the Arms placed on its Sides, with these eight Letters. *V. H. I. L. J. C. I. V.* underwritten. On a broad oval Circle, or Field, were written these following Words, *Born of God, died in JHSVH, sealed with the Holy Ghost, does rest here* Jacob Behmen *of* Old Seidenburg, *who, the seventeenth of* November, *about Six o'Clock in the Forenoon, in the fiftieth Year of his Age, blessedly departed.*

In the Midst under the oval field, upon the Tree of the Cross, stood a Lamb with a Bishop's Mitre, under a Palm-tree, by a Water-spring in a green Pasture, feeding among the Flowers; there stood the Word *VENI.*

On the South Side was painted a black Eagle on a high Rock, which trod with his Left-foot on the Head of a great Serpent folded together; in the Right-foot he held a Branch of Palm, and in his Beak the Branch of a Lily, which was reached to him out of the Sun; by that was written the Word *VIDI.*

On the North Side stood a Lion, having on his Head a Cross and a Crown, placed with his right Hinder-foot on a Cube, with the left on a Globe; in his right Fore-paw he held a flaming Sword, in his

Left a burning Heart; by him was written the Word *VICI.*

Upon the Tree of the Cross stood his last Words, *Now I go hence into Paradise.*

This hieroglyphical Monument would not have remained long, but have been razed and imbezzled by the rude Hands of the Envious, had they not been prevented by the Magistracy; for they would willingly have lavished their impotent Wrath against him, on this wooden Cross, and discovered their Hatred to the Memory of his Goodness, whom they would long before have crucified.

**Reverend William Law's
1764**

Copyright © 2019 / Alicia Éditions
Credit: Pixabay
All rights reserved

www.ingramcontent.com/pod-product-compliance
Lightning Source LLC
LaVergne TN
LVHW092008090526
838202LV00002B/50